Meaningful
Memories

Joseph N. DeLuca, MD, PhD.

BALBOA.
PRESS
A DIVISION OF HAY HOUSE

Balboa Press books may be ordered through booksellers or by contacting:

Balboa Press
A Division of Hay House
1663 Liberty Drive
Bloomington, IN 47403
www.balboapress.com
1 (877) 407-4847

Because of the dynamic nature of the Internet, any web addresses or links contained in this book may have changed since publication and may no longer be valid. The views expressed in this work are solely those of the author and do not necessarily reflect the views of the publisher, and the publisher hereby disclaims any responsibility for them.

The author of this book does not dispense medical advice or prescribe the use of any technique as a form of treatment for physical, emotional, or medical problems without the advice of a physician, either directly or indirectly. The intent of the author is only to offer information of a general nature to help you in your quest for emotional and spiritual well-being. In the event you use any of the information in this book for yourself, which is your constitutional right, the author and the publisher assume no responsibility for your actions.

Any people depicted in stock imagery provided by Thinkstock are models, and such images are being used for illustrative purposes only.
Certain stock imagery © Thinkstock.

ISBN: 978-1-5043-7849-9 (sc)
ISBN: 978-1-5043-7850-5 (e)

Print information available on the last page.

Balboa Press rev. date: 04/26/2017

Table of Contents

Acknowledgement..vii

Dedication...ix

Memorable Experiences I Had With My Father 1

When I Was Six 4

Speech Therapy 5

Who Is Sleeping Under The Stairwell Tonight 6

Why Do People Have To Die? 7

The Pain Of Having A Tragic Thing Happen To A Loved One 8

A Scar To Remember 9

Can We Do Yesterday Again? 10

The Candy Machine 11

You Are Going To Have To Pay For It Yourself............................... 12

Suck It Up 13

Homeless For Christmas 14

Jesse Owens 16

You're Starting Off, Six To Nothing, Against You 17

Pulling The Plug 18

A Moment Of Compassion 19

The Nursing Home 20

A Certain Part Of The Brain Never Dies... 21

Communicating Bad News 22

Things I've Learned From My Mother... 23

Beauty Is As Beauty Does.. 24

Having The Courage To Be A Nobody...25

Our Core – Our Inner Child...26

Role Playing In Kindergarten...27

It's Important To Have A Do-Over..28

Let's Replay Our History Of Past Positive Experiences..29

You're In!"...30

The Ecstasy Of The Journey..31

Things That Give Me Goose-Bumps...32

Readings To Enhance Insight Health, Wellness, And Positive Sentiments 35

Previous Books Published By Joseph N. DeLuca, MD, PhD 39

In Memoriam 41

Acknowledgement

I would like to thank my beautiful wife, Dr. Penny DeLuca for her help in editing this manuscript and for her enthusiastic support. In addition, I would like to thank Sharon and Ray Fields for their advice regarding formatting certain parts of the manuscript.

Dedication

I dedicate this book to all those who do an act of compassion each day,
You are the beautiful people of the world.

The Journey is the Reward

Tao Proverb

Memorable Experiences
I Had With My Father

Wrestling with him as a preschooler.

Teaching me how to ice skate.

Teaching me how to take a splinter out of my finger.

Going to his garage with him on Saturday mornings when I was young and watching him work on cars as an auto mechanic and explaining what he was doing.

Going to the diner next door at lunch time and having a ham sandwich. To this day it is my favorite kind of sandwich.

Taking me to the circus.

Taking me to a New York Yankee baseball game when I was in 5th grade.

I still remember the entire lineup.

Taking me to the World Series game between the New York Giants and Yankees

at the Polo grounds.

Taking me to see a game between the Brooklyn Dodgers and Cardinals at Ebbets Field.

Listening to the Notre Dame Football games on the radio on Saturday afternoons,

while I helped him wash his car

Watching the Friday night fights on TV with him.

Helping him build the upstairs to our house when I was in 8th grade.

Playing golf with him.

Playing ping-pong with him.

Watching football games on TV with him.

Taking me to my first NFL game between the New York Giants and Detroit Lions at Yankee Stadium.

Riding the waves at Jones Beach with him.

Taking me fishing on Long Island Sound where we caught lots and lots of flounder.

Watching him be affectionate and caring to my mother, as well as to my brother and sister.

Experiencing his great sense of humor. He was always the life of the party, telling one hilarious joke after another.

Watching his ability to work hard and long.

Playing the same violin that he played when he was in high school.

Having him teach me how to appreciate the violin virtuoso of Jascha Heifetz.

Discussing the importance of "respect" and "gratitude."

Teaching me how to ride a bicycle, drive a car, and change a tire.

Showing me how to shave.

Going to meet him in Manhattan at a steak restaurant. Then going to Madison

Square Garden to watch the New York Knicks beat the Boston Celtics in basketball.

It was a great evening. When it was over we hugged and said our good-byes.

I never saw him again

Tragically, two weeks later, he was killed in an auto accident.

He was 59 years old.

<u>Take away</u>

Savor each and every moment that you have with a loved one. You never know when that will be the very last moment that you will have with them.

When I Was Six

When I was six years old, in first grade, my father gave me a baseball glove. It was a Charlie "KingKong" Keller glove, who, at that time, was the left fielder for the New York Yankees. The only problem was that I was left-handed. My father didn't realize it, and the glove was for a right- handed person. However, there was something about that glove that I loved. I loved the feel of it, the smell of it, and the look of it. I did not want to give it up. So, I decided, that in order to keep the glove, I would become right handed. Every day, for one month, I did with my right hand, everything that I used to do only with my left hand. After one month, I was able to do everything quite well with my right hand that I used to do with my left hand. I was able to keep the glove. Charlie Keller became my favorite New York Yankee baseball player.

Take away

It's wonderful that the brain can be so flexible to enable us to learn new skills for whatever the reason is meaningful to us. I am still hard-wired as a lefty. Even though my right arm is bigger and stronger than my left hand, when lifting weights in the gym, they go up a little smoother with my left arm. I can write more legibly with my left hand. That may be why my writing with my right hand has always been considered atrocious.

Speech Therapy

When I was in second, third, and fourth grade, I was referred each year for speech therapy. Apparently I was not able to pronounce many sounds or words properly. Along with about five other students, once a week, we met with Mrs. Joseph, the music teacher. She made us do different exercises with our tongue, which I recall as being very hard to do. One day, in third grade, my teacher, Mrs. Garrett, said: "say the word "boil." I said to her what I thought was the word "boil," but she kept saying that I was saying "berhl." After repeated attempts she slapped me across my face and said that I was purposely saying "berhl, although I pleaded with her that I was saying "boil."

<u>Take away</u>

Sometimes, even though we are absolutely sure we are correct about something, maybe we really are not. Apparently I was not hearing things correctly. Although I must admit, Mrs. Garrett was a little harsh about it.

Who Is Sleeping Under
The Stairwell Tonight

When I was in elementary school, during the winter on three different occasions, upon leaving for school in the morning, I saw a homeless man who had been sleeping under the ground floor stairwell. He had apparently urinated on himself and the floor reeked from the strong stench. I always felt scared that he would wake up and run after me. So I would immediately run up to our second floor apartment and tell my mother about this man. I asked her why does he do that and she said to me in a very stern voice "That is because he refuses to get a job." I thought, wow, get a job and everything will be ok or sleep under a stairwell and pee all over yourself.

Years later, as an adult, I realized that most homeless people, even if offered a job could not work, due to mental illness or addiction problems. I see people a few times a week, holding up a sign begging for money and they always seem physically ok. They aren't in wheelchairs or on crutches and they appear to stand tall and walk normally. Maybe my mother was right. Maybe they feel that begging is their job. Maybe.

<u>Take away</u>

Perhaps there is an alternative explanation for everything.

Why Do People Have To Die?

When I was in fifth grade, one day I asked my mother, "Why do people have to die? " She said: "When people get very old, God wants them to be in heaven with him. " I said that why can't God make heaven come down here to earth so that we wouldn't have to feel so sad when someone we really like died. She said: "That sounded like a good idea, why don't you talk to God about that?" Well I did, but he never got back to me about it.

As an adult, I realized that God does give us a spritz or sprinkling of heaven throughout our lives. We all have had experiences where we felt "this is heaven, I feel like I'm in heaven, or this is so heavenly." So, we do get a sprinkle now and then of heaven on earth. However, I still wish God could make heaven come down here on earth, so we wouldn't have to feel so sad when someone we love dies.

Take away

We might think we have a pretty good plan for something. Perhaps someone knows better than us, why their plan is better.

The Pain Of Having A Tragic Thing Happen To A Loved One

My grandmother, a private duty nurse, was on her way to care for a sick and dying child at Mount Sinai Hospital in New York City. As she walked on her way there, she was smacked over the head with a blunt instrument by someone who robbed her pocket book. She died immediately of a massive brain hemorrhage. No doubt, this is one of thousands of examples of a person, endeavoring to do an act of goodness and caring meeting a tragic end.

Take away

It has always left a hole in my heart.

A Scar To Remember

One day during the summer vacation before 6th grade, I was running across the top of the concrete wall that separated my apartment house from the one across the alley. A friend of mine was also running on it, about ten yards ahead of me. The superintendent of the neighboring apartment house did not want any kids running on that wall. He came after me with a long wooden board that had a long nail at the end of it. He swiped it at me. As the nail tore through my pants, it caused a deep gash in my right buttock, which bled profusely. I was able to outrun him and climb down off the wall. When I got home I told my mother I had slipped and fell on broken glass. She had a look of skepticism about my explanation. I developed a three inch long scar from the wound. The scar has stayed with me my entire life.

Take away

Be grateful for the little scars in life. Had the nail in the board hit my spinal cord, I could have been paralyzed for life.

Can We Do Yesterday Again?

When I was in sixth grade, my family's finances improved significantly. My father bought a car, we had a TV, went on vacations, and food was very plentiful. On holidays we had many relatives come over to our house for huge dinners. One Easter weekend we had many relatives come over and there was great food and fun. The next day I asked my mother if we could do yesterday again. She said it would be hard for her to entertain many people each weekend. Maybe I should check with the other relatives and they might take turns having a big dinner for everybody each weekend. Well, I did check with each and every one of them and they all said they just weren't able to do it.

Take away

Even though you might have a good idea, it doesn't mean that others will be cooperative or supportive of it. If possible, just do it yourself.

The Candy Machine

When I was in 6th grade, I went to a movie at the Laconia theatre in the Bronx, New York. As was usual, I first went to the candy machine. When I arrived there, a frail, young-looking African-American boy was standing in front of the case. He said to me that he put his money in the machine, but could not get the candy to come out. He showed me which candy bar he was trying to get out. I gave the lever a very hard yank, and the candy bar dropped down into the tray. I handed it to him. He smiled, and ran away.

Take away

I still remember that incident. I can only think that even the simplest act of helpfulness can be the prototype for future acts of kindness.

You Are Going To Have
To Pay For It Yourself

When I was in eighth grade, I passed the admission test for the private high school, Archbishop Stepinac in White Plains, New York. This school was about twelve miles from my home. My father preferred that I go to the local public school, which was only three blocks away. He said that if I was serious about going to that school, I would have to pay for it myself. I continued my weekend lawn mowing business, got a paper route and was able to make the monthly tuition payments without any trouble the first year. My father said that since I had proven that I was serious, and had done very well academically, that he would take over the tuition payments from that point on.

During my senior year in high school, I applied to a private college, Notre Dame in Indiana, which was a thousand miles from my home in New York. My father said he thought I should live at home and commute to a local college in order to save money. Again, he said, if I was serious, I would have to work summers to help defray the cost of college and I agreed to do so. We went on the tuition plan, which enabled us to make monthly payments. In addition, I got money from joining the Army ROTC, and worked part-time as the athletic director of a YMCA that was close to my college. During my Junior and Senior years in college, I qualified as a tutor and earned five dollars a session tutoring philosophy, physiology, and zoology. During each summer I worked full time and continued my weekend lawn mowing business.

Take away

It's good to work hard to pursue your dream. The journey is definitely the prize.

Suck It Up

One day at high school football practice, as the quarterback, I was told to run a certain play in the scrimmage that was taking place. The play involved me faking a hand-off to the right half-back, going off of right guard, and then having the option to pitch out to the left half-back, bellying around the right end, or keeping it myself and running into the defensive backfield. I decided to take the latter option. About five yards into the defense, I got hit simultaneously by three defenders, one on each hip, and one on my lower right leg. I heard and felt a crunch in my right hip and fell to the ground in pain. In those days, in the early 50's, unless your leg was sticking thru your skin or you were unconscious, you were expected to "suck it up," jump up and run back to the huddle. I acted as though I wasn't in any pain and jogged back to the huddle. Thankfully, that was the last play of the scrimmage and practice was over. However, as an adult, I developed arthritis in that hip as a reminder of that "suck it up" moment. I even remember hearing the football coach say to the assistant coach that he thought one of my teammates had suffered a concussion, but since he seemed ok. "It shouldn't be a problem."

Take away

Thanks to improvements in medical diagnosis and treatment, whenever a player is injured, he or she is immediately evaluated. This is especially important if a concussion is suspected. One can have serious, possibly long term consequences if not properly treated immediately

Homeless For Christmas

When I was in college at Notre Dame in Indiana, in order to get home for Christmas vacation I hitch-hiked 1,000 miles each way from my campus to where I lived in New York. I did not have the money for a plane, train, or bus and in 1958 this mode was considered relatively safe. It usually worked out pretty well; I would leave campus and get a ride to the Indiana Turnpike. From there I would stand outside the rest stop and tell people that I was a Notre Dame student trying to get home for Christmas. Could they please give me a ride to the last rest stop just before they got off the Turnpike? Then, I would go from the Indiana Turnpike into the Ohio Turnpike, onto the Pennsylvania Turnpike, and then the New Jersey Turnpike, until I finally managed to make it into New York. It usually took about a day and a half. In my junior year, just before Christmas vacation, I decided to spend a few days in Indiana visiting my girlfriend. After the visit I arrived back on campus on the evening of the 22nd. I left early in the morning of the 23rd anticipating I would make it home late on the 24th. I got a ride to the Indiana Turnpike. It took until late that day to get onto the Ohio Turnpike. On the evening of the 23rd I got a ride from an Oriental couple who said they were going to the end of the Ohio Turnpike. I told them to let me off at the rest stop, before they got off the turnpike. I apparently fell asleep in the back of their car. When I awoke I discovered they had forgotten to stop and leave me off at a rest stop. We were in the middle of nowhere, on a lonely road 10 miles from the turnpike. I guess with our language barrier they misunderstood my request. I told them to let me out and I proceeded, on a cold and windy night to walk the 10 miles back to the turnpike. No cars stopped for me on this dark narrow road. At dawn on the 24th I got a ride to a rest stop at the beginning of the Pennsylvania turnpike and promptly fell asleep in the rest stop for six hours. When I awoke, it was late afternoon on the 24th. I called my parents collect and told them I was alright, but it might take another day or two to get home. I remember hearing my grandmother crying, in the background, and telling my father that he should go and get me. (I was only five hundred miles away from home, one way) Rides were getting few and far between, and I did not get to the end of the Pennsylvania Turnpike until the evening of the 24th. It took me until late on the 25th to get to the New Jersey turnpike. With few rides available I did not make it into New York until the morning of the 26th. Upon arriving home I slept for 24 hours. There is nothing like spending Christmas on the New Jersey turnpike.

Take away

Plan for unforeseen circumstances before embarking on a long and important trip.

Jesse Owens

When I was a senior in college, and a member of the Notre Dame Track team, we travelled to the University of Chicago to participate in a multi-college track and field competition. After competing, my teammates and I sat in the infield, when Jesse Owens walked over to us and starting talking. I ended up talking to him, one on one, for about five minutes. I had never met anyone famous that was as nice as Jesse. I remembered seeing videos of him on TV, over the years; Jesse winning his four gold medals at the 1936 Olympics in Berlin and Hitler walking out of the stadium as this African-American man from the US dominated his Aryan athletes. Previously, Hitler had said that "blacks and Jews are not real people". On the way back to campus I told our track coach. Alex Wilson, about my conversation with Jesse. He said that many years before, as a member of the Ohio State track team; Jesse came to Notre Dame to compete in a dual meet. The next day at practice, I went to the starting line of the 100 meter dash. I crouched down into the start position of the 100 meter sprint hoping to find out if Jesse's spirit was still in one of the lanes. I don't know why, but of the eight lanes I tried, I sensed Jesse's spirit in lane number seven.

Take away

Goodness and greatness can often co-exist.

You're Starting Off, Six To Nothing, Against You

I applied to medical school when I was 41 years old. I thought I had a favorable chance of being accepted, as I had scored at the 92nd percentile on the Medical College Admissions Test, had a high GPA from a prestigious college, as well as being a board certified PhD in Clinical Psychology. I told the person who was interviewing me that I wanted to take an interdisciplinary view of patients and view them as a whole person, rather than just the psychological or physical. At the end of the interview, the doctor, a gastroenterologist, said he wanted me to know that there were 17 people on the admissions committee, four of whom were PhD's who had never voted for another PhD and two were medical students who had never voted for anyone over 30 years old, so "you will be starting off 6-0 against you." Two weeks later when I received the letter from New Jersey Medical School, informing me that I had been accepted as a medical student. I was overwhelmingly and pleasantly surprised.

Take away

Never give up hope even though some people may have
a bias against you for irrational reasons.

Pulling The Plug

When I was a first year, Internal Medicine resident, on call with my team, I was told that I was designated to disconnect a particular patient from life support. I felt really uncomfortable about it, so I carefully checked his chart, and indeed, two independent neurologists had declared him brain dead. In addition, all the other paper work, such as end of life documents were in order. So, about 8:30 pm I disconnected him from his life support, and assumed he would probably stop breathing shortly thereafter. I went back to his bedside every thirty minutes and for the next two hours he continued to breathe on his own with a regular heartbeat. At around the third hour, upon examining him, his heart had stopped beating and breathing had ceased. I pronounced him dead, but kept thinking that maybe if he had been kept on life support he might have been the one out of a thousand who, after weeks or months in a coma, started breathing on their own. I know I did the correct action, but I have never felt comfortable about it.

Take away

Sometimes doing the right thing, feels like the wrong thing.

A Moment Of Compassion

I'm a Primary Care Physician and a Clinical Psychologist. About one year ago, along with their staff member, I had two mentally retarded adults come to my office for a routine medication mental health management session. One person was a woman in her 40's and the other was a man in his 50's. As I was talking to the woman, the man, who was sitting next to her, began having a panic attack and was visibly shaking. The woman immediately stood up, went over to him, and while putting his hands in hers she said in the most loving and caring voice, "it's OK, everything is going to be OK." He immediately stopped trembling and completely calmed down. I was very touched by the degree of compassion that this woman showed to him.

Take away

The most important part of a person is their heart. Compassion outweighs all other possible assets or abilities that a person has. The most important things in life come from the heart.

The Nursing Home

About twice a month I go to a nursing home and do a guardianship evaluation for a patient considered not able to make rational decisions regarding any or all personal and financial matters. The person has usually been diagnosed with Alzheimer's Dementia and I am asked to assess cognitive functioning and give an opinion regarding their degree of impairment. As I walk thru the halls of most nursing homes, the strong stench of urine pervades the premises. In addition, there are often, huddled before a TV, a group of 15-20 patients who are slumped over in their wheelchairs, often drooling, and unaware of the TV or their surroundings. It just seems so sad that this is the end of life care and daily existence for these patients. I realize it is for good reason, that because their families are unable to care for them, that the nursing home is the only alternative. I don't have the answer. Maybe having volunteers interact with these patients offering some kind of social stimulation might be a partial solution.

Take away

There must be something we can do to prevent simple "warehousing"
of our impaired seniors.

A Certain Part Of The Brain Never Dies

As said, I perform many guardianship evaluations in nursing homes,

Usually the individuals have been diagnosed with dementia. Many were very high functioning individuals before they became debilitated. An example was a patient who had been an engineer, having worked for NASA for many years. Upon finishing the evaluation, the patient's wife, who had been in the room, said "isn't he a good-looking man." I replied that he certainly was, and that if the Hooter's girls found out about him they would want to come and visit. Well, upon hearing this he perked up, smiled, and gave me a "thumbs up." He knew exactly what I was talking about, whereas prior he could not calculate the simplest arithmetic problems. Not long after that episode, I had a lady in her mid- 80's come into my office. She was diagnosed with dementia. In the presence of her daughter, the women said to me "can you send over to my house any good-looking men? " I told her that I was not able to do that and I then said to her "if I sent over to your house today 2 good-looking men and then 3 good-looking men the next day, how many good-looking men would that be altogether. "She immediately said 5; whereas previously she could not tell me how much was 2 plus 2.

Take away

I think the implication is that certain parts of our brain continue to function well regardless of diagnosis. If we blend in rational thinking by pairing it up with that part of the brain that holds emotionally meaningful things, we may be able to slow down the progression of dementia. It's certainly worth a try. I read a study years ago whereas boys, who had difficulty learning to read, were paired it up with readings that interested them, such as sports. The results showed this method enabled them to learn to read fairly well. So I think there is something to pairing up rational thinking with whatever is emotionally meaningful to the person.

Communicating Bad News

About two to three times a year I need to tell a patient that their test results, either an MRI, CAT Scan, blood work, or other tests, showed the possibility of a life threatening medical problem. I try to tell them in the most calm, caring manner possible, and tell them that I will be referring them to a specialist who will tell them further information about the treatment and prognosis for their condition. I feel that each of my patients is like a member of my family and communicating bad news in as caring a manner as possible is important.

<u>Take away</u>

It is very painful for the patient.
It is very painful for me.

Things I've Learned From My Mother

My Mother taught me what unconditional love was all about. As an extremely sensitive, caring, and affectionate person, she was always hugging, kissing, and telling us how much she loved us. She was so very sweet and compassionate, that she cried easily when touched by someone's difficulties.

My mother was very intelligent and determined. She finished two years of college during the Great Depression, while working as an assistant to a history professor, as well as having part time jobs as a dental assistant, and a model. As a voracious reader, she would go through the Book of the Month Club book every two weeks.

She was generous and hard working. From my 5th grade on, she made huge meals every holiday for most of our relatives. My son Stephen still remembers the aroma of wonderful Italian red sauce, "gravy," that permeated, whenever he walked through the front door of my mother's home.

My mother had a flare for design and color. Our house was beautifully decorated, both inside and outside. The garden was amassed with brilliant and aromatic roses. After my father died, she became a certified interior decorator.

My mother had a subtle wise-ass sense of humor with a touch of sarcasm. For example, her way of communicating was to say ask: "Tell me again why you chose a sport where the goal of the opposition is to bash your head in?"

And my mother had unbelievable confidence that I could do or accomplish anything that I wanted to do. For example, when I told her that I was surprised, because of my age (41 years old) that I was admitted to Medical School. She said, "Why, do you think that was actually going to be hard for you?"

Take away

It was such a blessing to see and feel unconditional love.

Beauty Is As Beauty Does

Having conducted many men's psychotherapy groups over the year's one issue always came up. Men would say that if they were dating someone who was physically attractive and she began to act like a "psycho-bitch "that they started to look physically unattractive. On the contrary, men often said that if they were dating someone who was very ordinary looking, but was so nice, they appeared to become physically attractive. So, no doubt, beauty is as beauty does. Research has shown that if a person smiles it enhances their physical attractiveness by two-fold and if they frown or look cranky it detracts from their physical attractiveness by four-fold. Moreover, apparently, standing or walking tall enhances a person's physical attractiveness.

Take away

Walk tall and smile to enhance your physical attractiveness. Needless to say, beauty is as beauty does and handsome is as handsome does.

Having The Courage To Be A Nobody

In his book <u>Franny and Zoey,</u> J.D. Salinger describes a trip that Franny takes to visit an Ivy League College for a weekend. While there, she notices that just about everyone is bragging about all of the things that they had accomplished and all of the things that they plan to be very successful in. She felt very turned off by their narcissistic rantings. On the train ride back to New York City where she lived, she says to herself, that the one thing that she would like to accomplish in life is to develop the courage to be "a nobody."

<u>Take away</u>

Develop yourself in every way, but to display it as Narcissistic Personality Disorder is definitely a turn off

Our Core – Our Inner Child

The experiences we have as a child form a core of our personality and persist throughout adulthood. Our inner child influences everything we do, feel and how we react and perceive life experiences.

Take away

Getting in touch with our inner child is the key to understanding ourselves.

Role Playing In Kindergarten

It would appear that the role of compassion in daily life is so important; it should become part of the educational curriculum. One important step in this process would be the use of role playing, starting at the very latest in kindergarten. Each day, the teacher would spend some time having the children rehearse how and what they would say depending upon the situation that required an act of compassion, whether it was an animal or a person that was hurting, injured, or in need of a caring, sympathetic, empathetic, and the helpful behavior on the part of the child learning the act of compassion.

Take away

It's never too early to educate for the most important thing in life.

It's Important To Have A Do-Over

Everyone has had experiences where, upon looking back at them, wish they could have handled it differently. It could be something they should have said, or not said, or said or did in a different way. It is usually helpful to replay those incidents, either in your imagination or in reality, but this time, say and or do what would have been the ideal thing to have done. This helps reintegrate the experience into a positive one.

Take away

Everyone deserves a do-over.

Let's Replay Our History Of Past Positive Experiences

Like the song says, "Thanks for the Memories." We all have a ton of memories that were wonderful and replaying them will enhance our since of wellbeing.

Take away

We should express our gratitude to those that made special memories possible.

You're In!"

In 2002 at the National Championships in Masters Olympic Weightlifting, I exceeded the qualifying total to participate in the World Championships in Melbourne, Australia. I knew that each country was only permitted to send a limited number of lifters, even though they met or exceeded the qualifying total for their weight class. So, after the competition I asked the USA weightlifting coach, Howard Cohen, how long it would take for him to decide who the lifters would be that he had chosen to go to the World Championships. He looked me straight in the eye and said "You're In! " I could have hugged and kissed him. Things worked out pretty well. I went to Australia and was fortunate to beat the lifter from Switzerland for the bronze medal in my weight and age class, earning the USA team 3 points, which enabled us to beat the Russians for the World Team Championship by one point. It was a very satisfying experience.

Take away

Be grateful to all those who give you a special opportunity to
participate in something special and memorable.

The Ecstasy Of The Journey

Whenever I had a goal, whether it was academic, athletic or otherwise, it often was a long-term goal that was years away. For each day, week, or month, that I made progress toward that goal it was pure euphoria. Even though reaching the goal was the climax, the thousands of progressions toward the goal were extremely exhilarating. It always seemed the journey toward the goal was the most emotionally satisfying part of any goal.

Take away

Enjoy the journey. That is the true satisfaction.

Things That Give Me Goose-Bumps

The Cello of Yo-Yo Ma,

Intermezzo from Cavalleria rusticana,

The voice of Enya,

The voice of Aine Minoque,

The bass clarinet of Acker Bilk,

Sarah Brightman and Andrea Bocelli singing "Time to Say Good-Bye."

Georgia Kelly's harp.

The guitar of Tony Mottola.

Gregorian chant.

Beethoven's Eroica

Watching a thorough-bred, race-horse walk; the ultimate combination of strength, speed, grace, and being of high spirit.

Delivering a baby.

Watching a mother hold her new born baby for the very first time.

Watching a toddler and a dog snuggle together

Listening to the Bee-Gees.

Louie Armstrong singing "Till there was you."

Watching the West Point Cadets march on their parade grounds Saturday morning with the marching band playing …

The Aria from Madame Butterfly, "Un bel di vedremo."

Ray Charles singing "America the Beautiful,"

Watching a funeral at Arlington National Cemetery,

Reading the letter that said I had been admitted to Notre Dame,

Reading the letter that said I had been accepted to medical school,

Remembering the first time I laid eyes on my beautiful wife, Penny.

Holding each of my five children, moments after they were born.

The Journey is the Reward
Tao Proverb

Readings To Enhance Insight Health, Wellness, And Positive Sentiments

Albom, Mitch. (2003, 2006) The Five People You Meet in Heaven

Albom, Mitch. (2009-2011) Have a Little Faith: A True Story

Albom, Mitch. (2006, 2008) For One More Day

Albom, Mitch. (2015) The Magic Strings of Frankie Presto: A Novel

Albom, Mitch. (2002, 2008) Tuesdays with Morrie: An Old Man, a Young Man, and Life's Greatest Lesson

Alexander, Eben. (2112) Proof of Heaven- A Neurosurgeons Journey into the Afterlife

Brown, Daniel James. (2013) The Boys in the Boat: Nine Americans and Their Epic Quest for Gold at the 1936 Berlin Olympics

Byrne, Rhonda. (2007) The Secret

Chapman, Gary. (2014) The 5 Love Languages: The Secret to Love that Lasts

Chopra, Deepak. (2011) The Seven Spiritual Laws of Success: A Practical Guide to the Fulfillment of Your Dreams

Chopra, Deepak. (2009) Reinventing the Body, Resurrecting the Soul: How to Create a New You

Colvin, Geoff. (2008) Talent is Overrated: What Really Separates World-Class Performers from Everybody Else

Dyer, Wayne. (2016) Living an Inspired Life: Your Ultimate Calling

Dyer, Wayne. (2005) The Power of Intention: Learning to Co-create Your World Your Way

Dyer, Wayne. (2009) There's a Spiritual Solution to Every Problem

Eagleman, David. Incognito-The Secret Lives of the Brain

Emerson, John (2016) Kevin Durant: From Underdog to MVP-When Hard Work Beats Talent. The Inspiring Life Story of Kevin Durant-One of the Best Basketball Players

Frankl, Viktor E. (1997) (1969) Man's Search for Meaning

Gladwell, Malcom. (2007) Blink: The Power of Thinking Without Thinking

Gladwell, Malcom. (2008) Outliers, The Story of Success

Greeson, Janet. It's Not What You're Eating, It's What is Eating You

Guanieri, Mimi. (2006, (2007), (2010) The Heart Speaks: A Cardiologist Reveals the Secret Language of Healing

Hall, Stephen S., (2010) (2011) Wisdom-From Philosophy to Neuroscience

Hendrix, Harville. (1988) (2001) (2008) Getting the Love You Want: A Guide for Couples

Lipton, Bruce. (2005) The Biology of Belief: Unleashing the Power of Consciousness, Matter and Miracles

Pausch, Randy. (2008) The Last Lecture

Pearsall, Paul. (1999) The Heart's Code: Tapping the Wisdom and Power of Our Heart Energy

Pearce, Joseph Chilton. (2010) The Biology of Transcendence: A Blueprint of the Human Spirit

Salinger, J.D. (1991) Franny and Zooey

Sawin, Leslie, Lionel Corbett, Michael Carbine. (2014) C.G. Jung and Aging: Possibilities and Potentials for the Second Half of Life

Schroeder. Gerald L., (1998) The Science of God: Convergence of Scientific and Biblical Wisdom

Spencer-Wendel, Susan and Bret Witter. (2013) Until I Say Good-Bye: My Year of Living with Joy

Tolle, Eckhart. (2006) A New Earth: Awakening to Your Life's Purpose

Weiss, Brian. (1996) Many Lives, Many Masters: The True Story of a Prominent Psychiatrist, His Young Patient, and the Past Life Therapy That Changed Both Their Lives

Weil, Andrew. (2005) Healthy Aging-A Lifelong Guide To Your Physical and Spiritual Well-Being

Zhi Gang, Sha. (2010) Soul Mind Body Medicine: A Complete Soul Healing System for Optimum Health and Vitality

Previous Books Published
By Joseph N. DeLuca, MD, PhD

Inspirational Sentiments to Become a Better Person, A Starter Manual (2013)
    –Published by Strategic Book.

Snippets, Memories to Enhance Healing, Health, and Wellness (2013)
    –Published by Balboa Press.

Snippets, Memories to Enhance Healing, Health, and Wellness – Second Edition (2015)
    –Published by Tate Publishing.

Snapshots of Life Changing Experiences and a Few Cranky Sentiment (2016)
    –Published by Tate Publishing.

The above books can be obtained through the websites of BarnesandNoble.com and/or Amazon.com

In Memoriam

A few months ago, I lost my dear friend Billy. We had been friends since we were four years old. We sat next to each other in kindergarten and had wonderful times together throughout our elementary school years. I moved out of our neighborhood the summer before eighth grade and we pretty much lost touch at that time. He went on to Harvard and became a well-known author, aka: William Melvin Kelley, writing best-selling novels all of which I did read with great pleasure admiring his ability to be such a great writer. During the past few years, Billy as well as two other dear friends from childhood, John and Sal, got together once a year in Ney York City, as I would come up from Florida to meet them in a restaurant. We would replay many of the things we experienced in childhood together with great joy in reliving them. Billy was a kind, gentle, and gifted soul. I miss you Billy.

I love you man.

Printed in the United States
By Bookmasters